Finger Exercises

for the Viola

Book Two

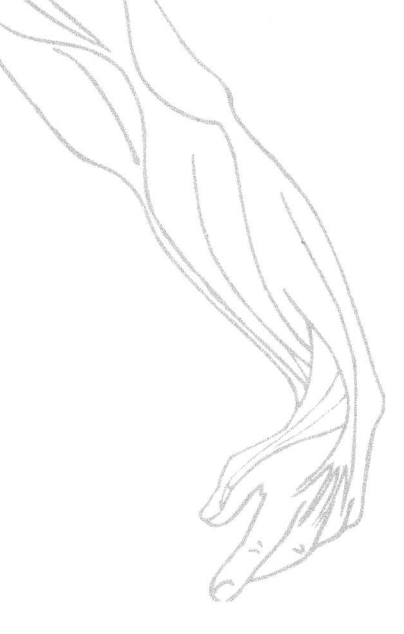

by Cassia Harvey

CHP323

©2018 by C. Harvey Publications All Rights Reserved.
www.charveypublications.com

Finger Exercises for the Viola, Book Two

1

Low First Finger

Cassia Harvey

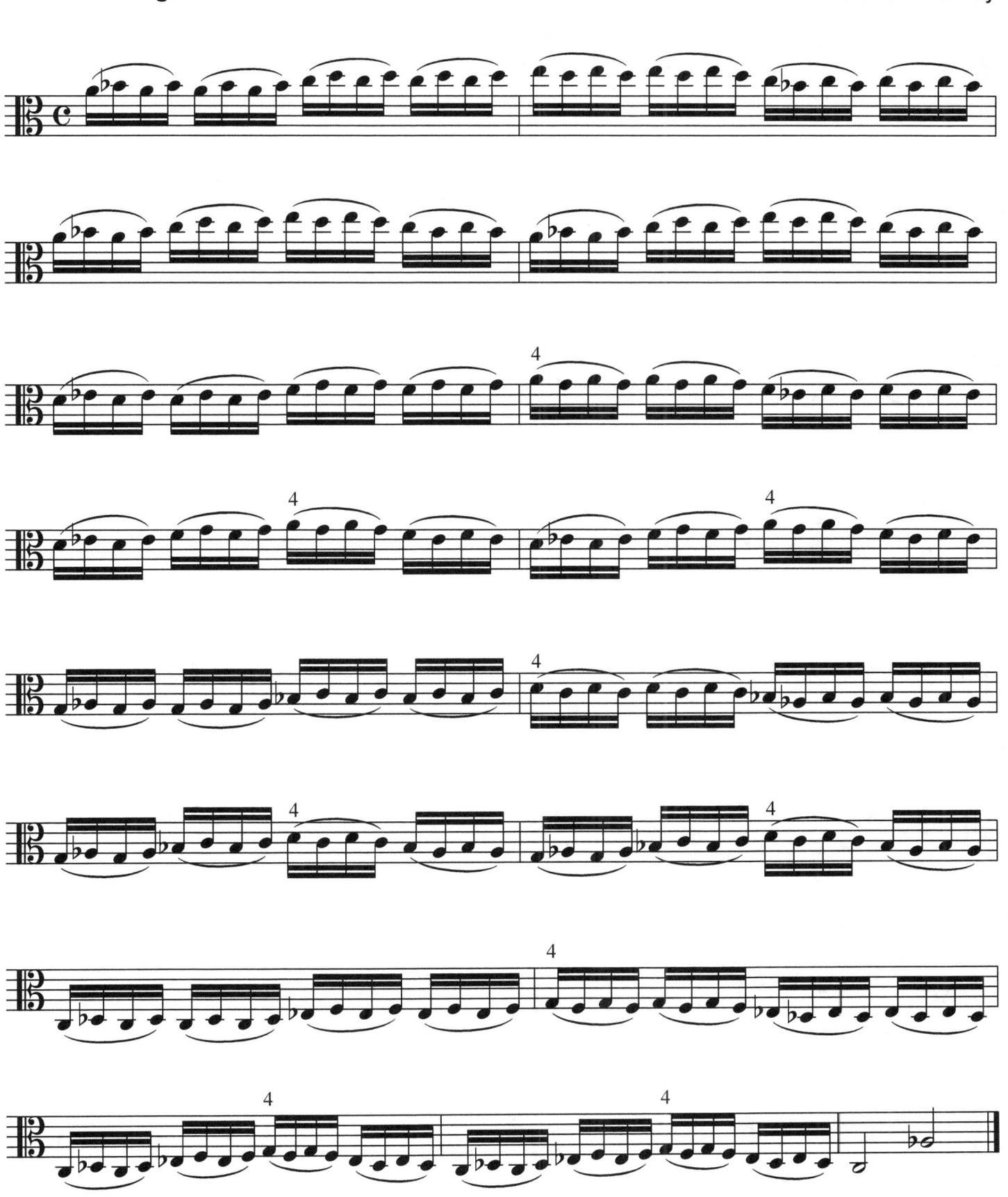

©2018 C. Harvey Publications All Rights Reserved.

2

Finger Exercises for the Viola, Book Two

3

4

Finger Exercises for the Viola, Book Two

5

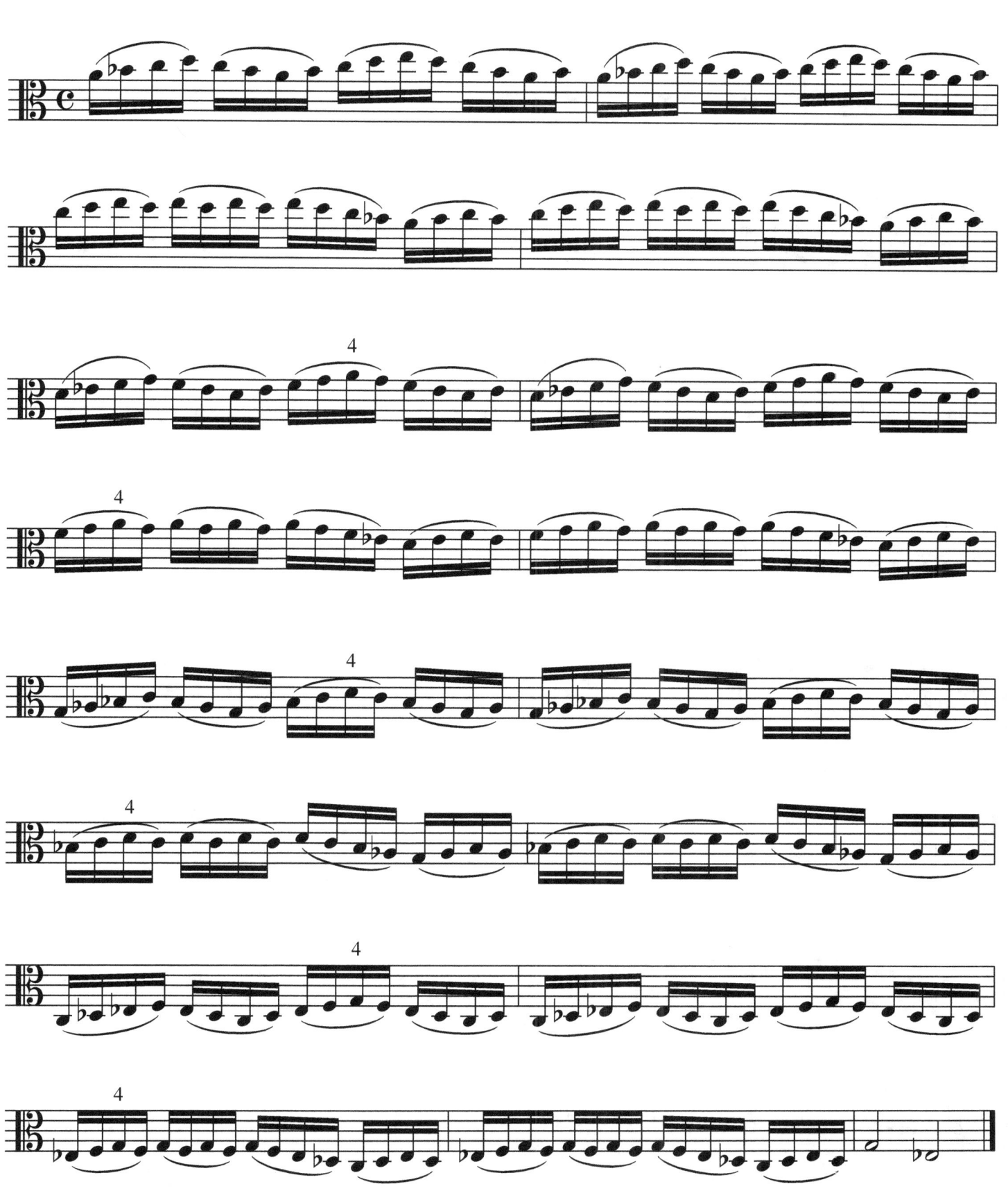

6

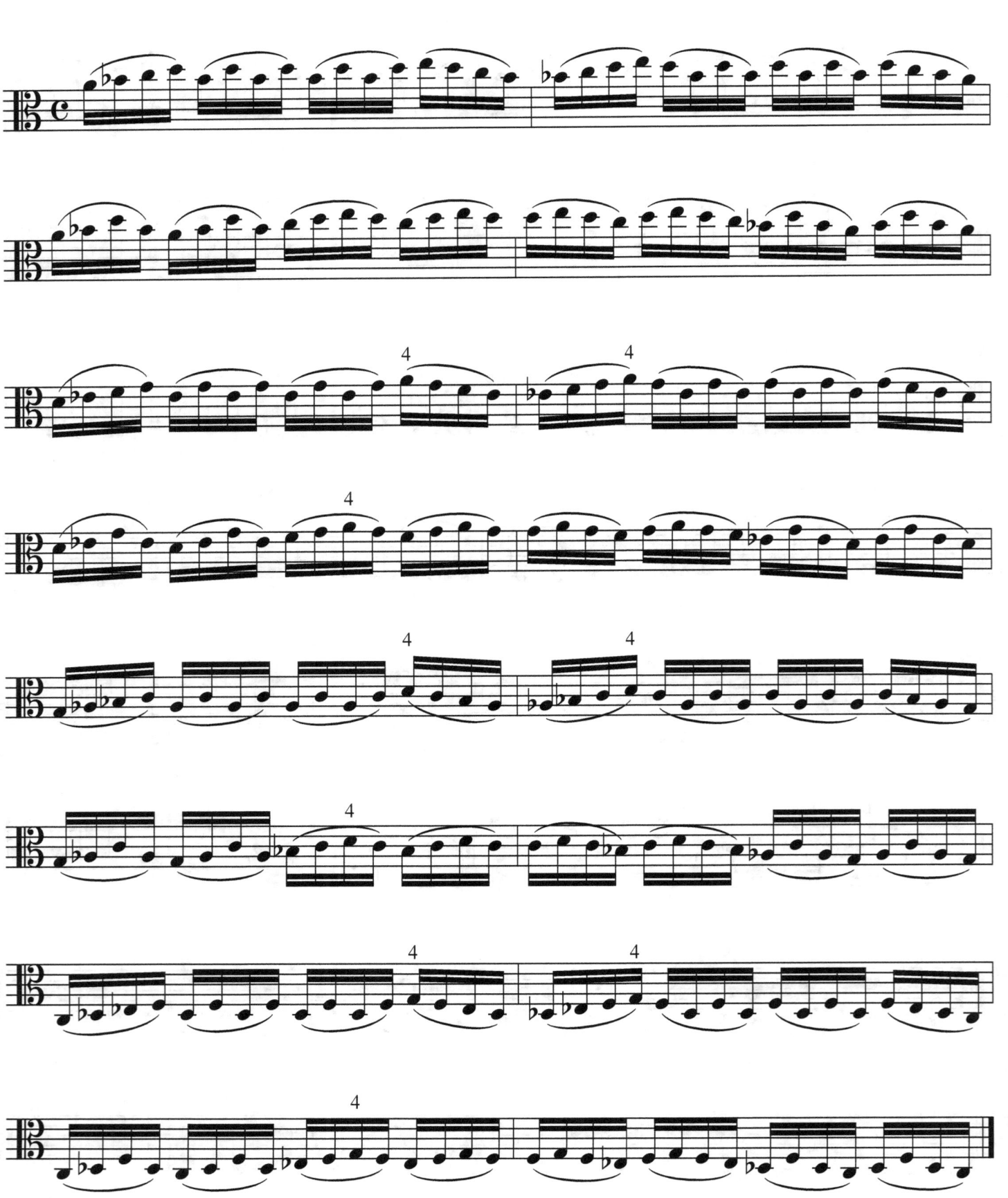

Finger Exercises for the Viola, Book Two

7

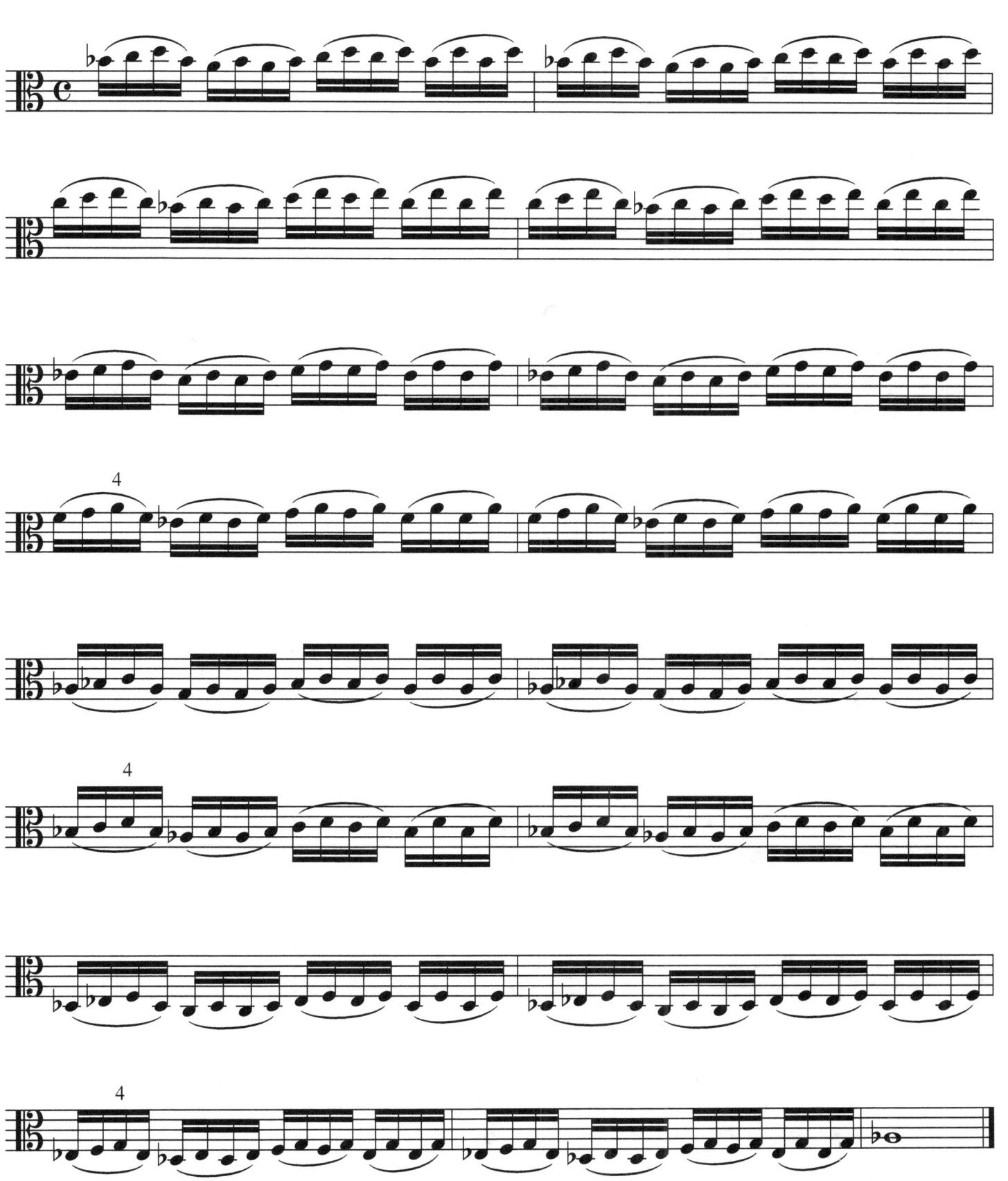

8

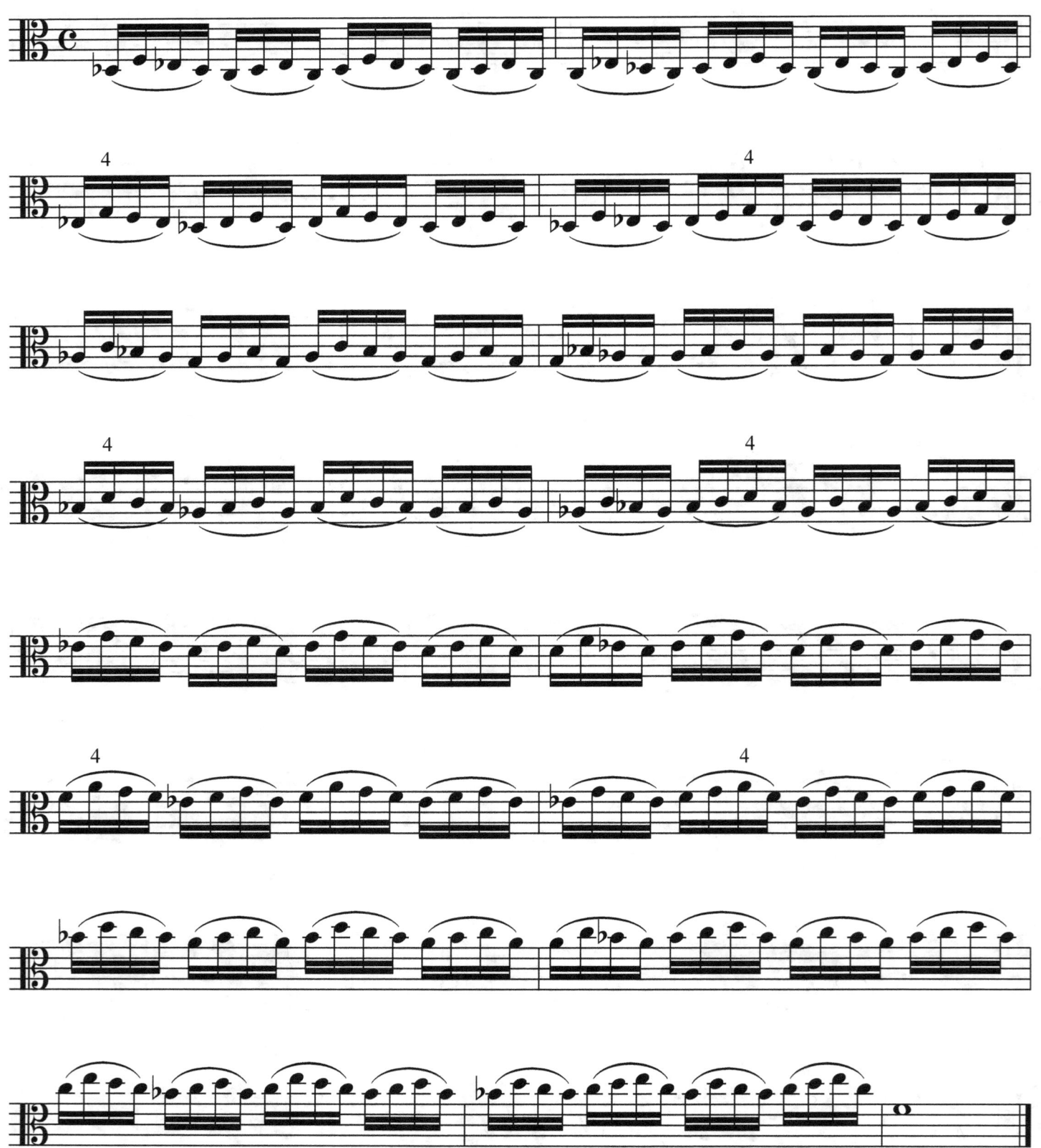

Finger Exercises for the Viola, Book Two

9

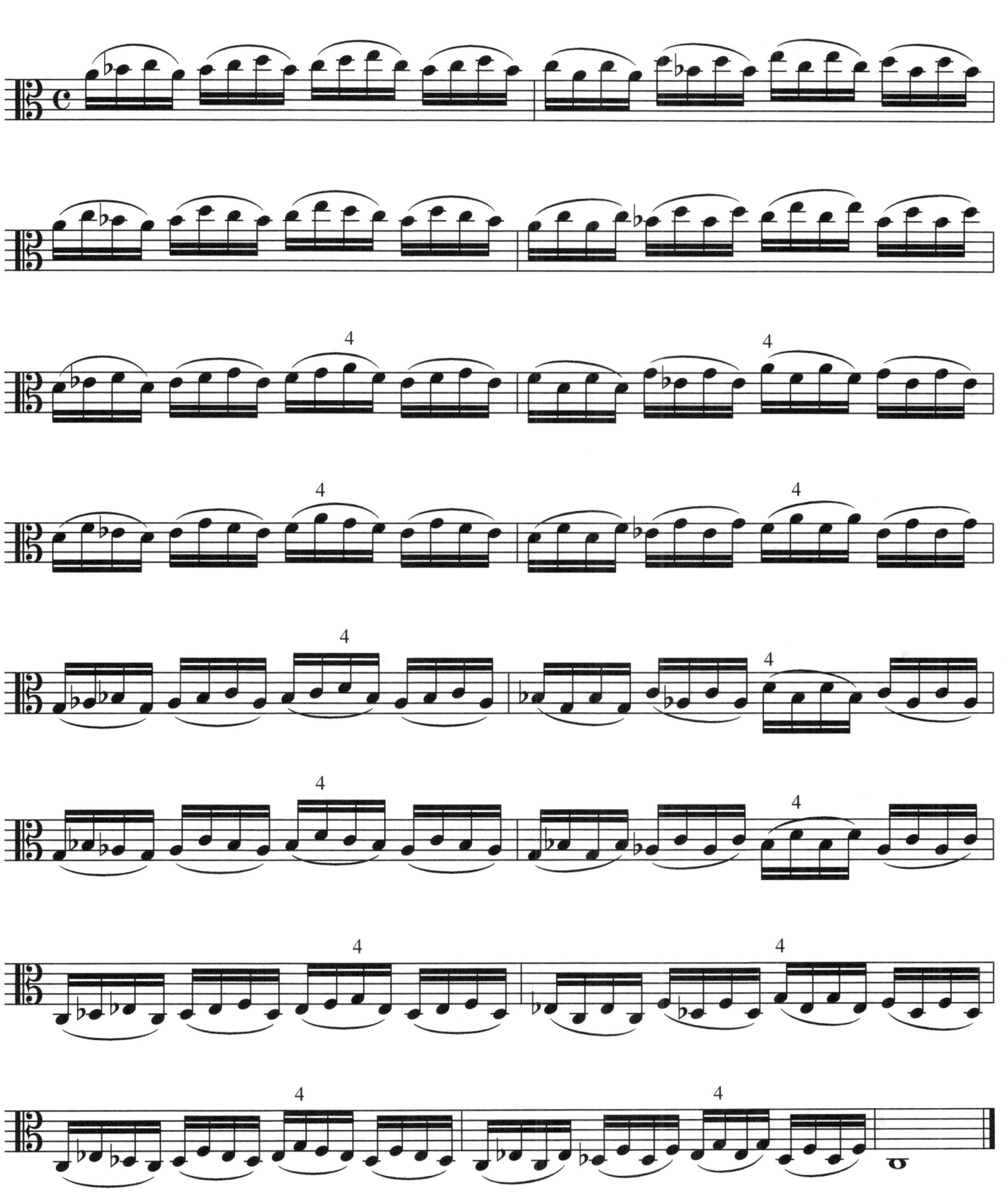

©2018 C. Harvey Publications All Rights Reserved.

10

Finger Exercises for the Viola, Book Two

11

High and Low First Finger

12

Finger Exercises for the Viola, Book Two

13

14

Finger Exercises for the Viola, Book Two

15

Low First Finger and Low Fourth Finger

Finger Exercises for the Viola, Book Two

17

18

Finger Exercises for the Viola, Book Two

19

20

Finger Exercises for the Viola, Book Two

21

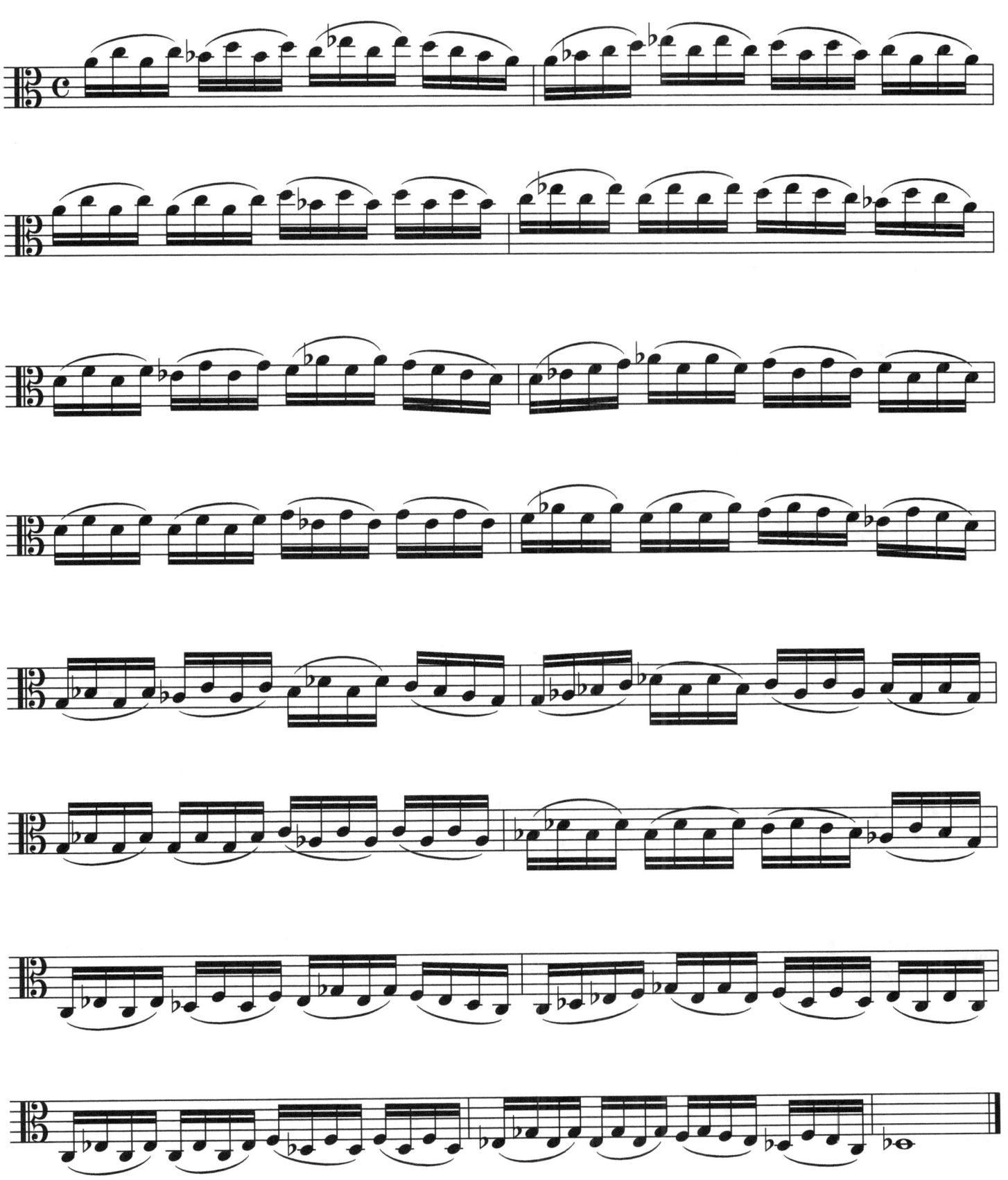

22

Finger Exercises for the Viola, Book Two

23

24

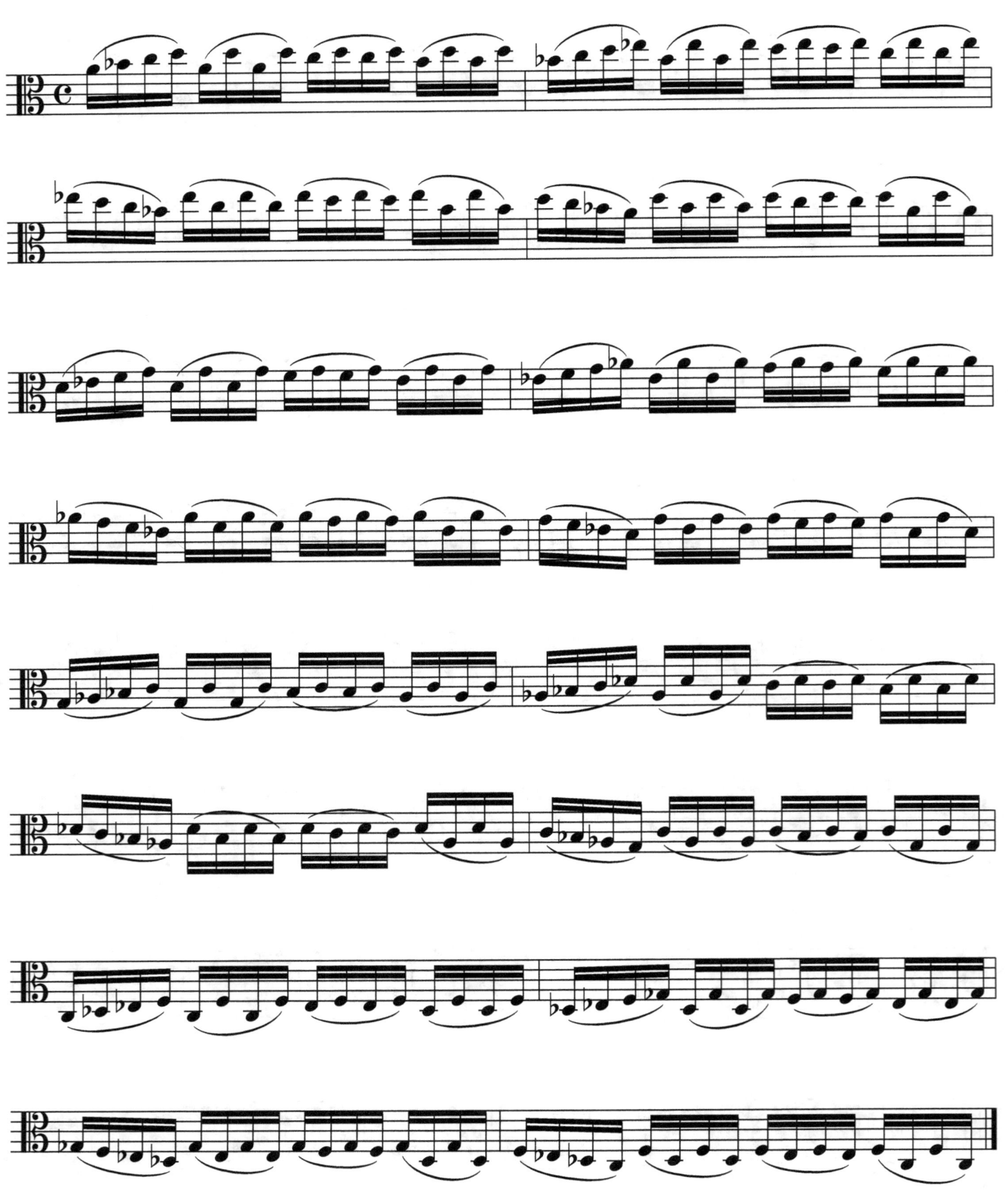

Finger Exercises for the Viola, Book Two

25

26

**High and Low First Finger
with Low Fourth Finger**

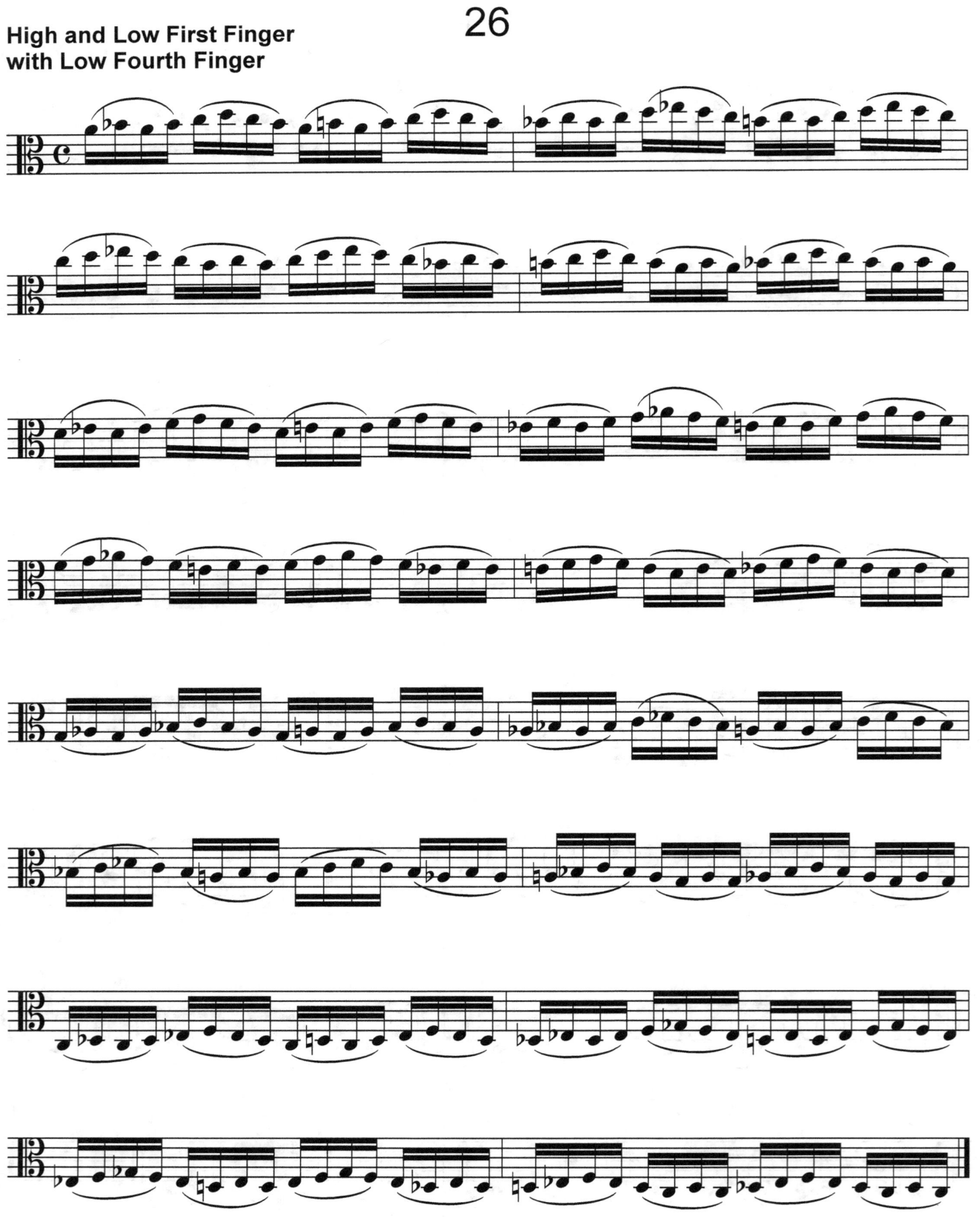

Finger Exercises for the Viola, Book Two

27

28

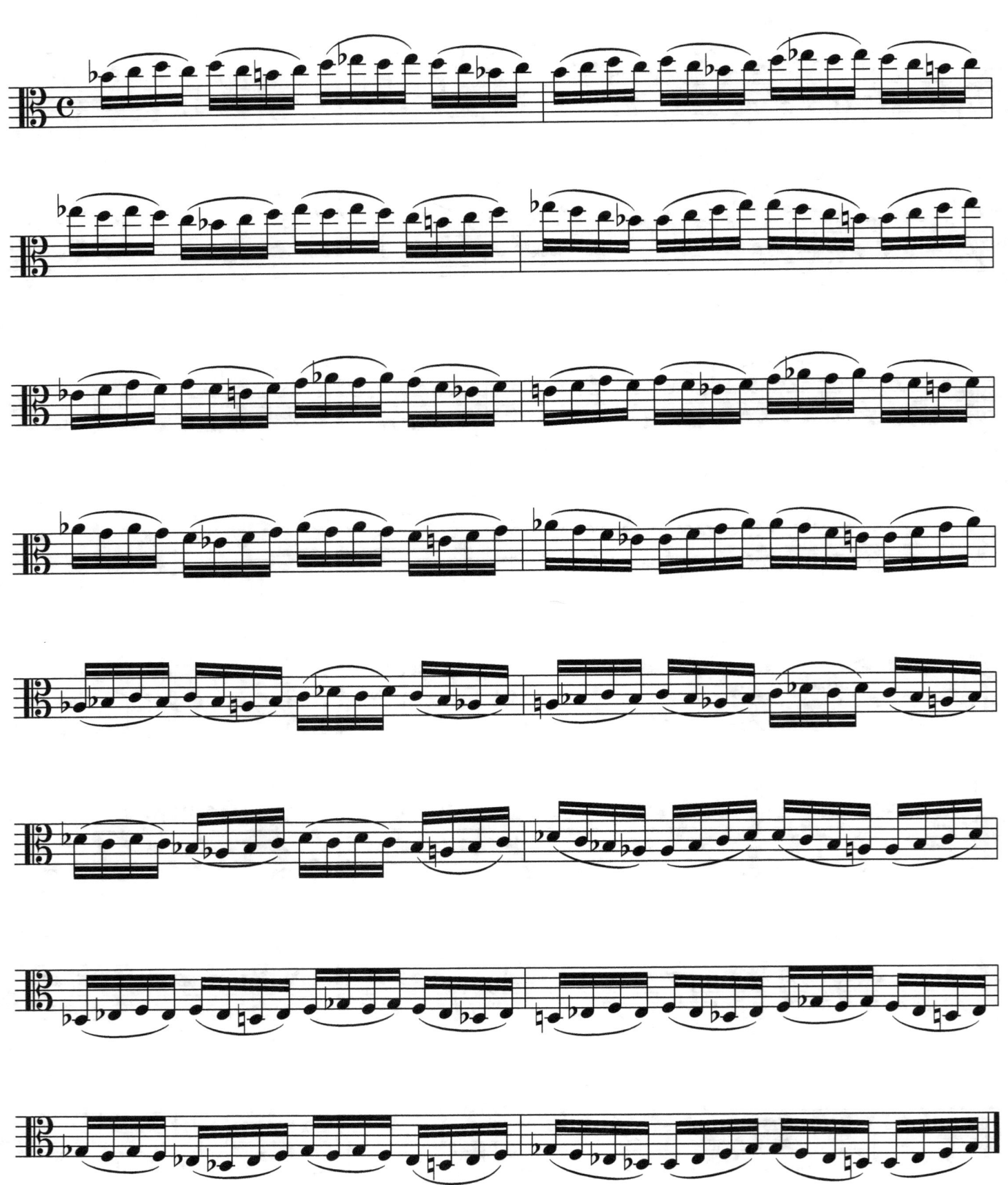

29

30

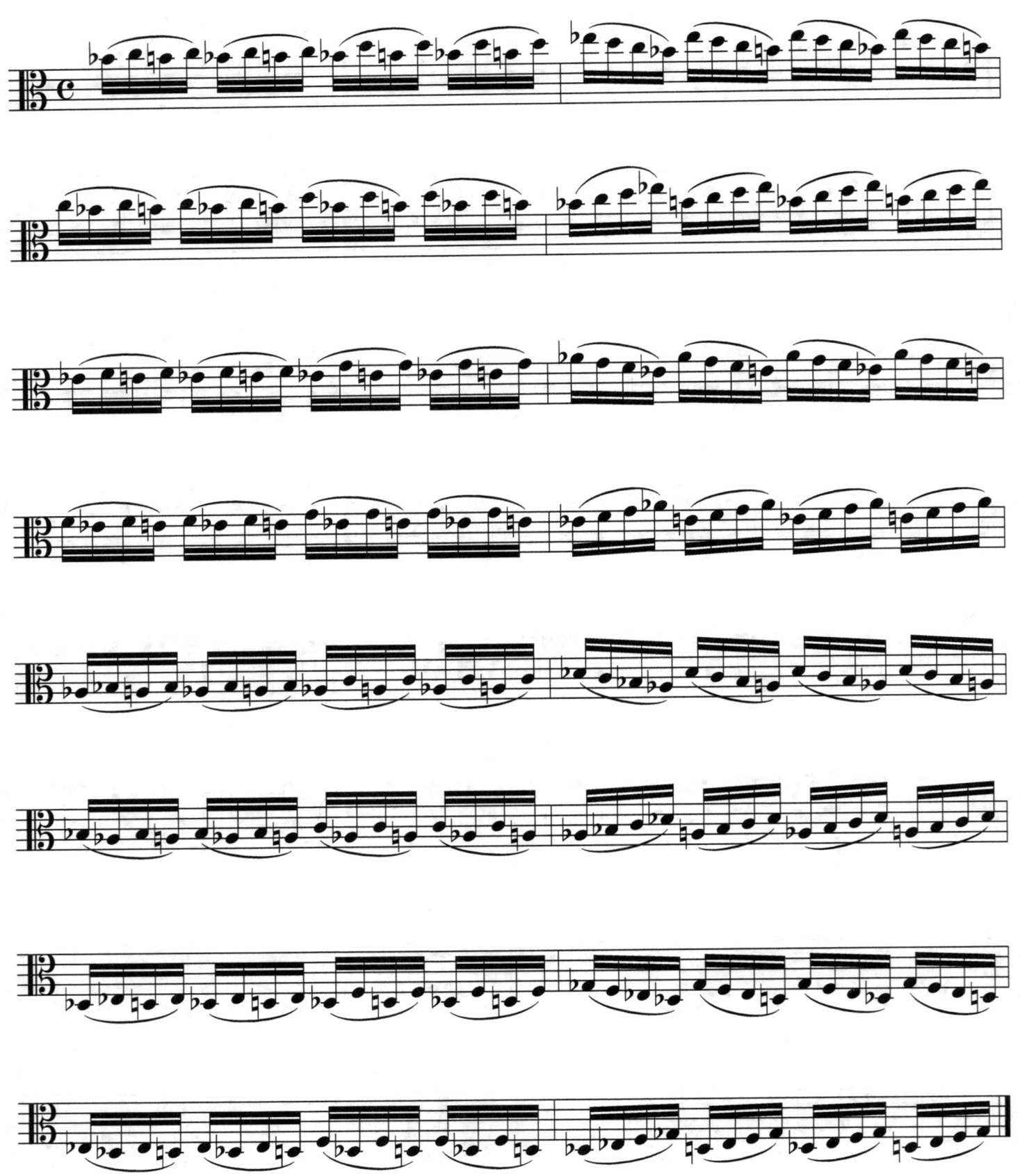

Finger Exercises for the Viola, Book Two

31

Low First, Third, and Fourth Fingers

©2018 C. Harvey Publications All Rights Reserved.

32

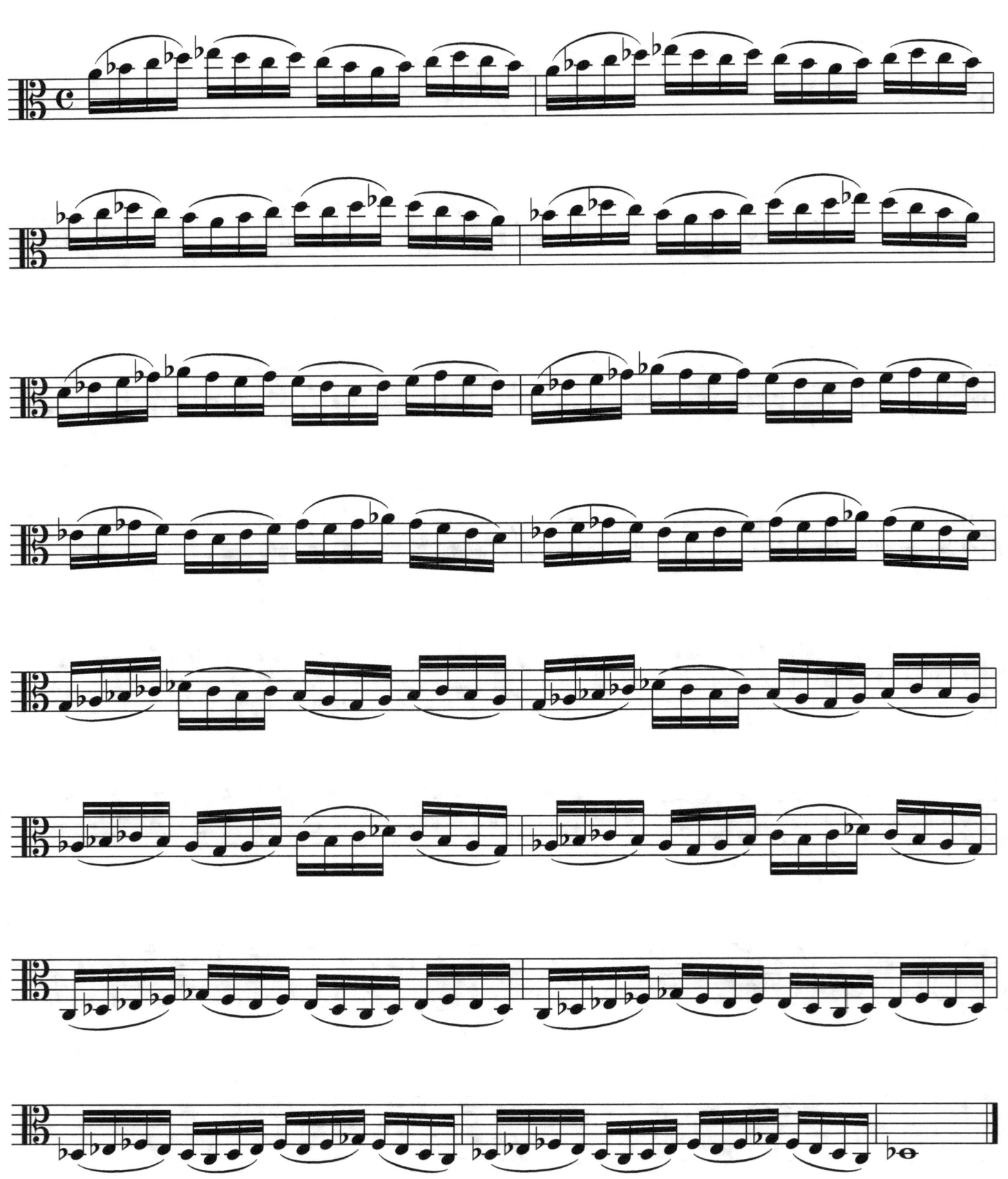

Finger Exercises for the Viola, Book Two

33

©2018 C. Harvey Publications All Rights Reserved.

34

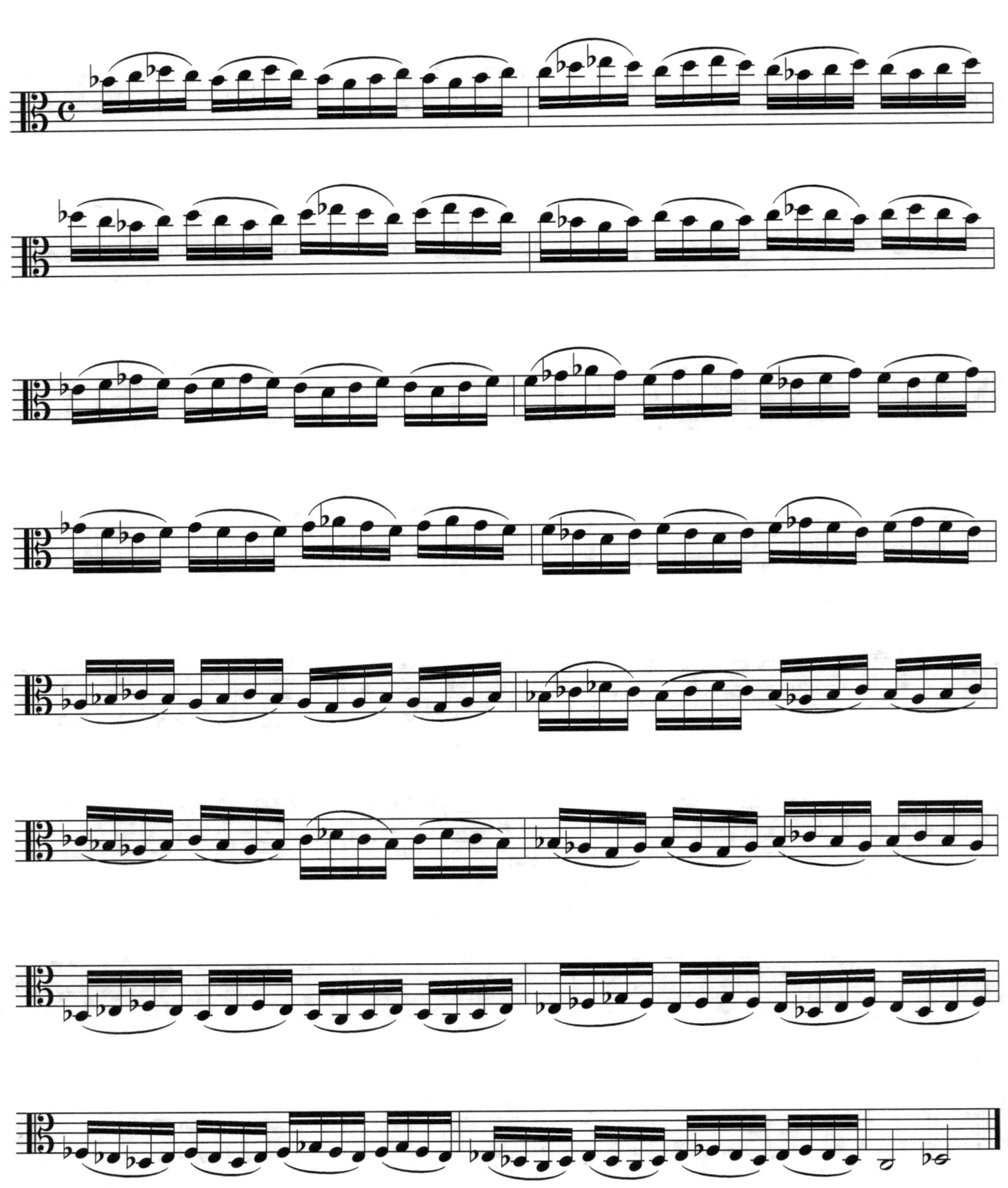

Finger Exercises for the Viola, Book Two

35

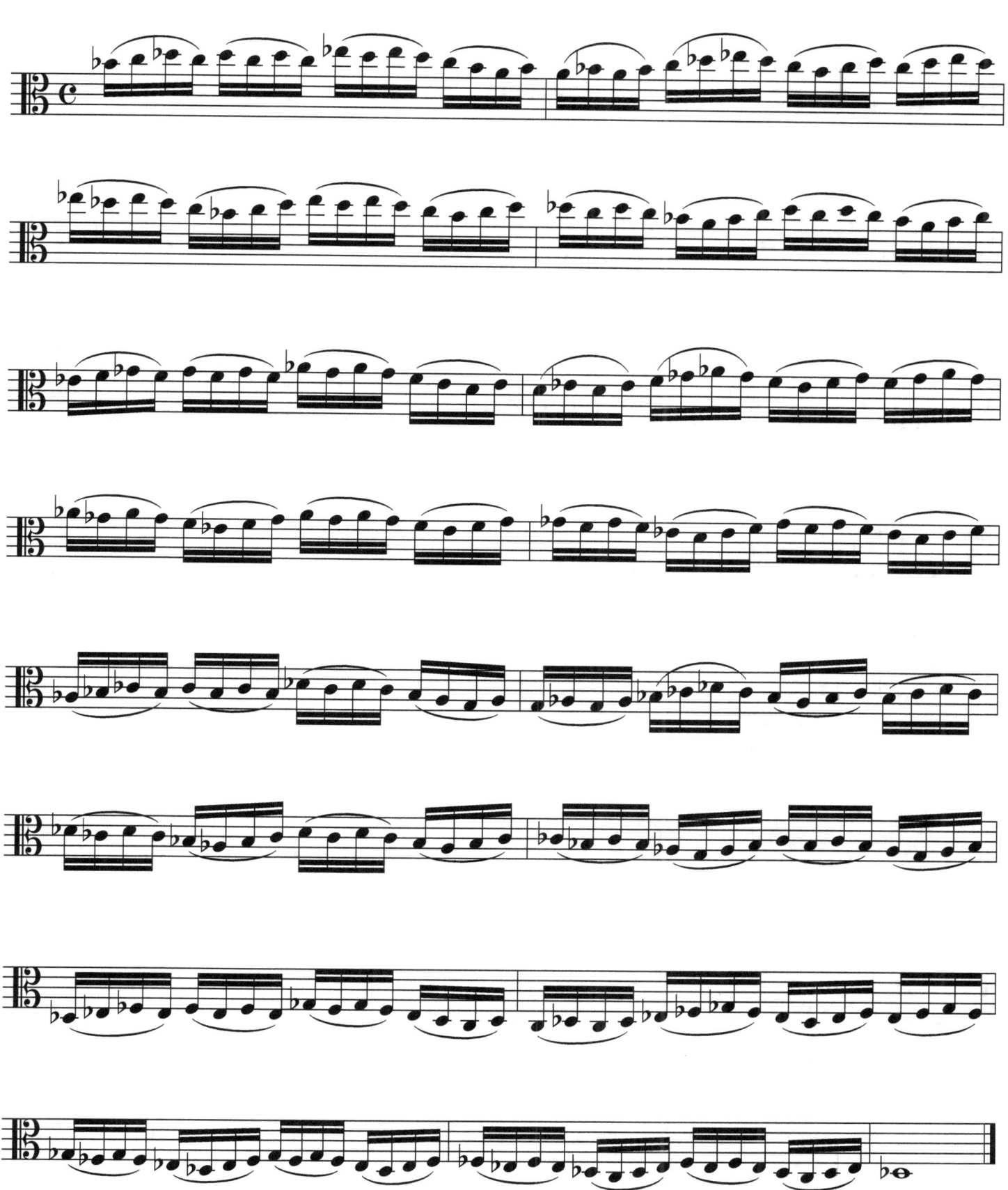

36

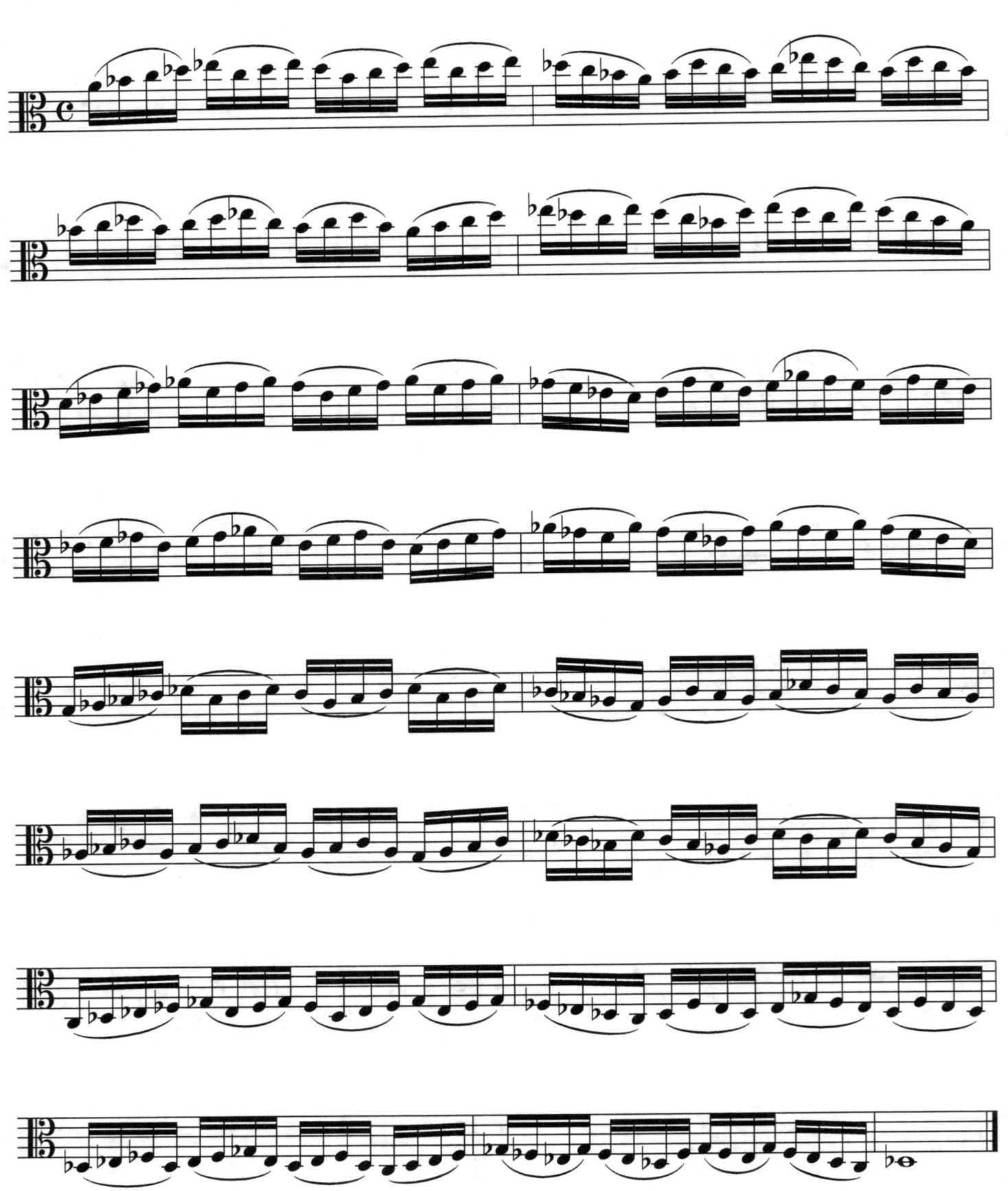

Finger Exercises for the Viola, Book Two

37

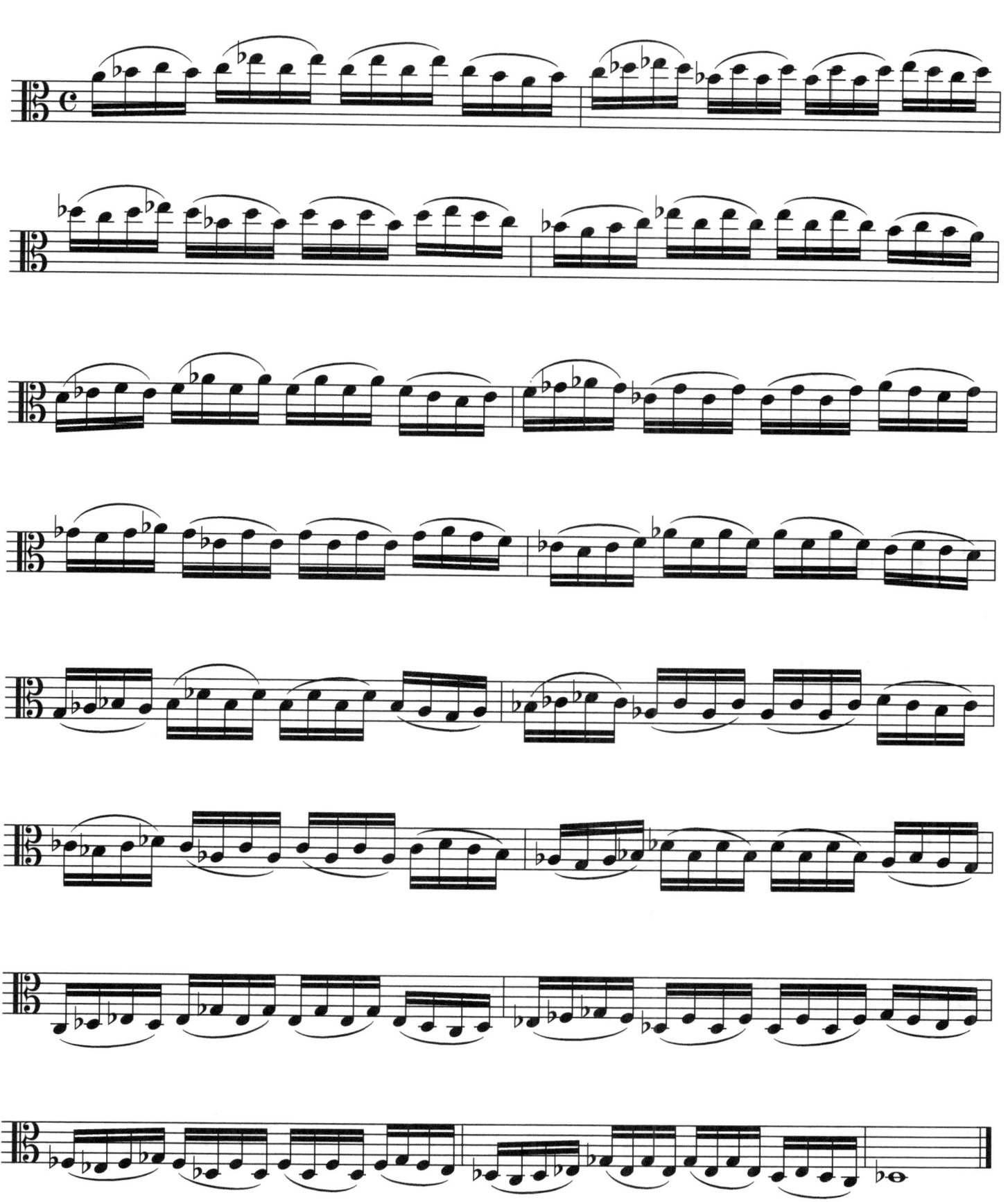

38

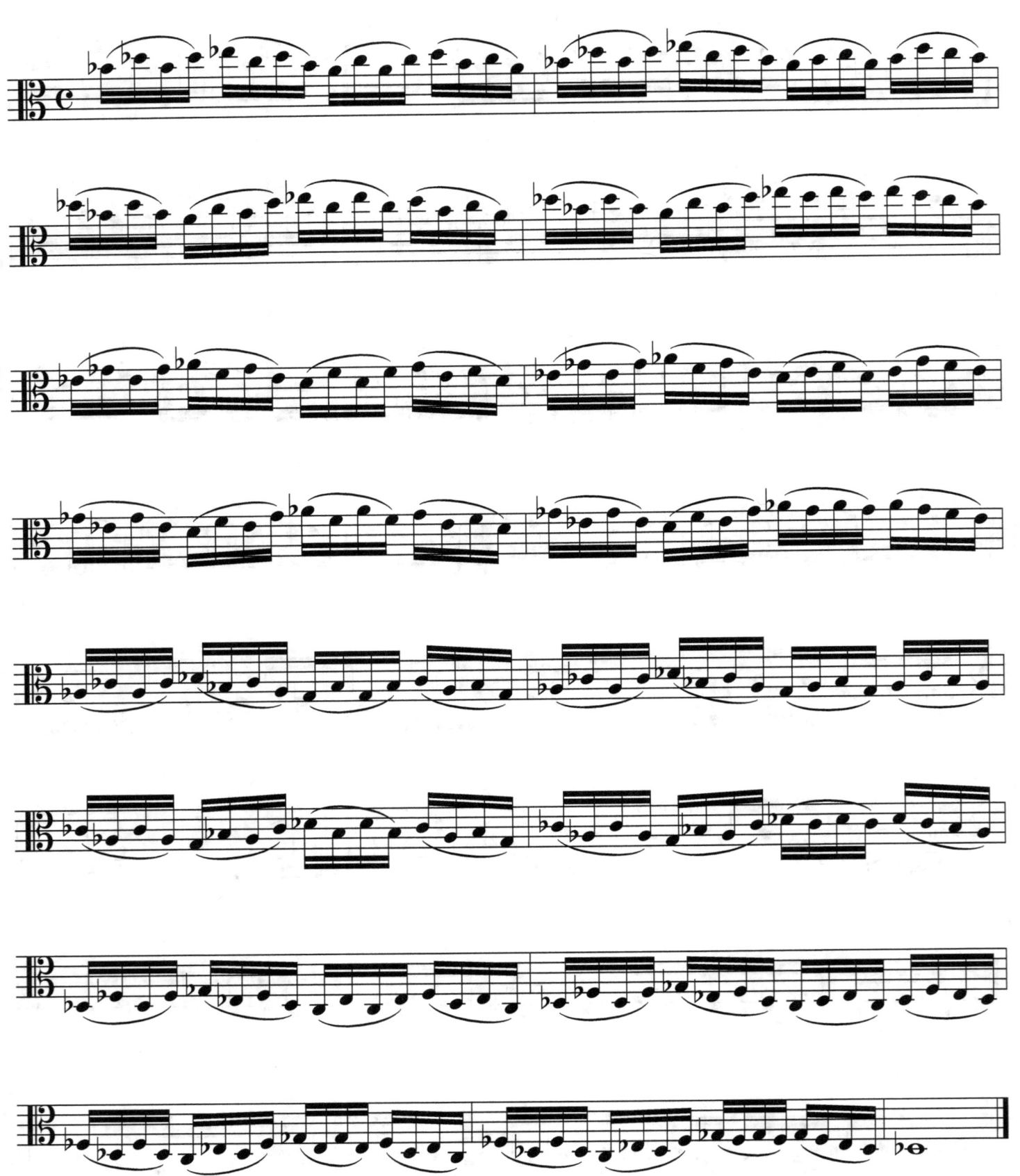

Finger Exercises for the Viola, Book Two

39

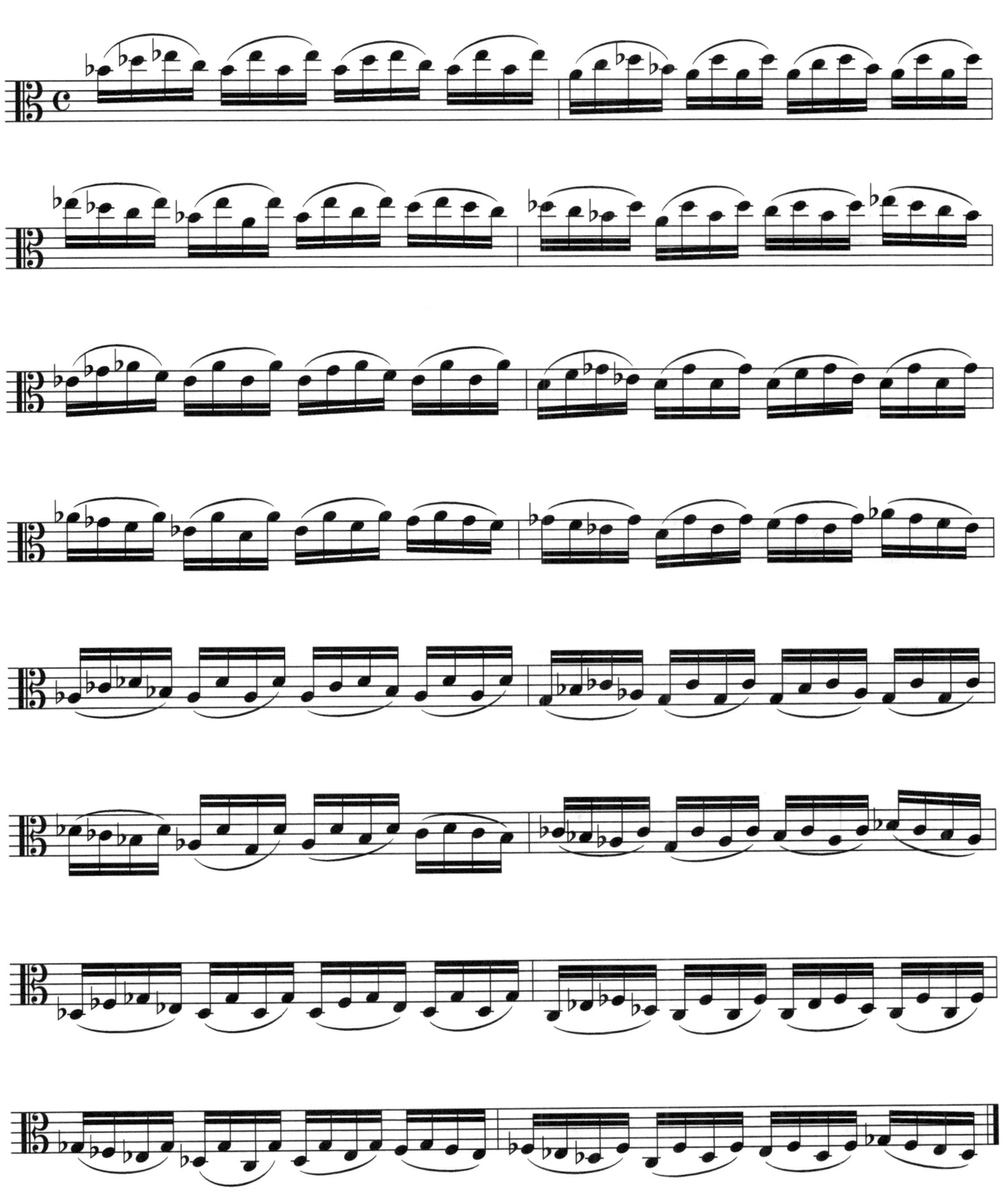

©2018 C. Harvey Publications All Rights Reserved.

40

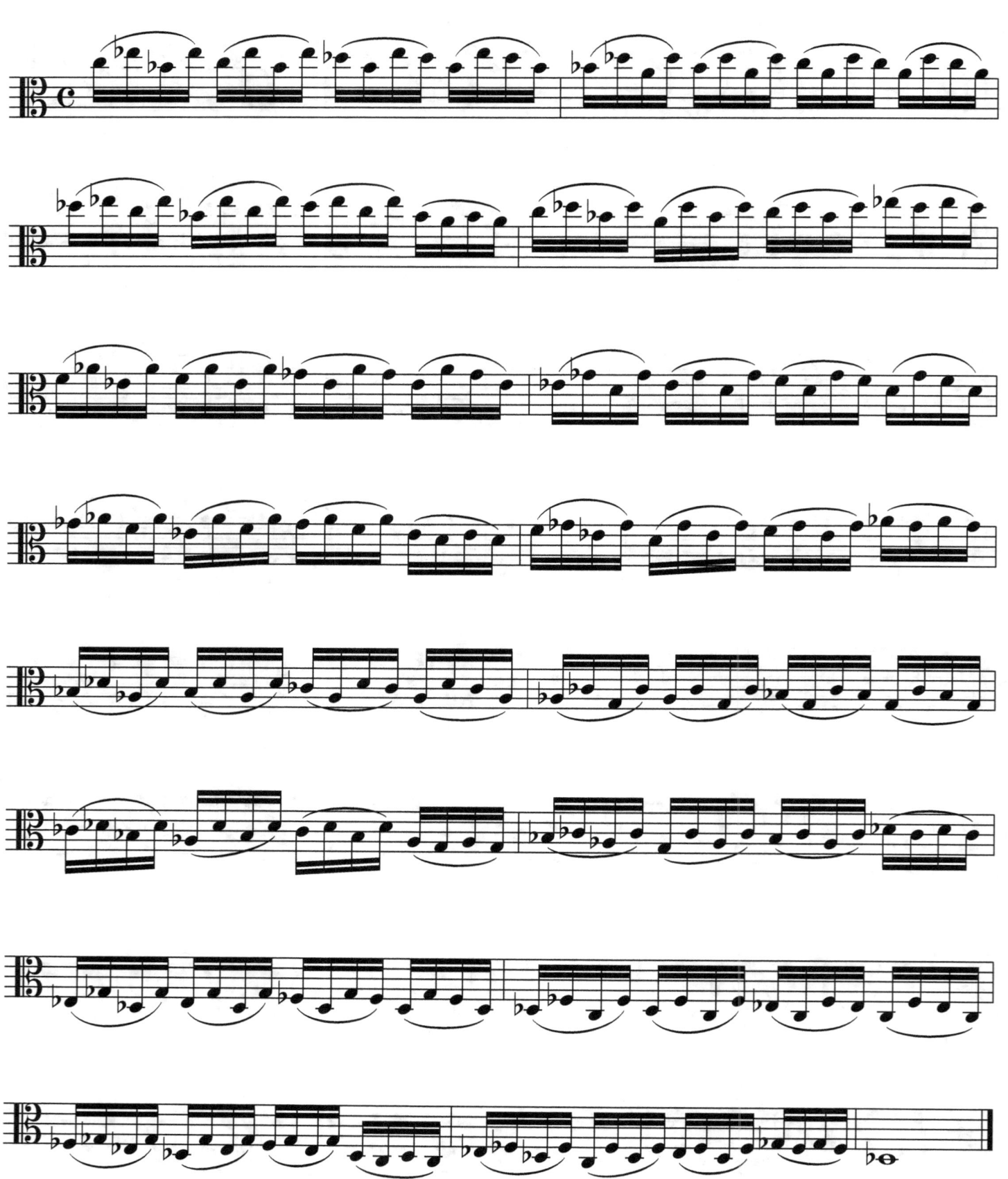

Finger Exercises for the Viola, Book Two

41

**Low First and Fourth Fingers,
High Second Finger**

©2018 C. Harvey Publications All Rights Reserved.

42

Finger Exercises for the Viola, Book Two

43

44

Finger Exercises for the Viola, Book Two

45

46

Low First Finger, High Second Finger

Finger Exercises for the Viola, Book Two

47

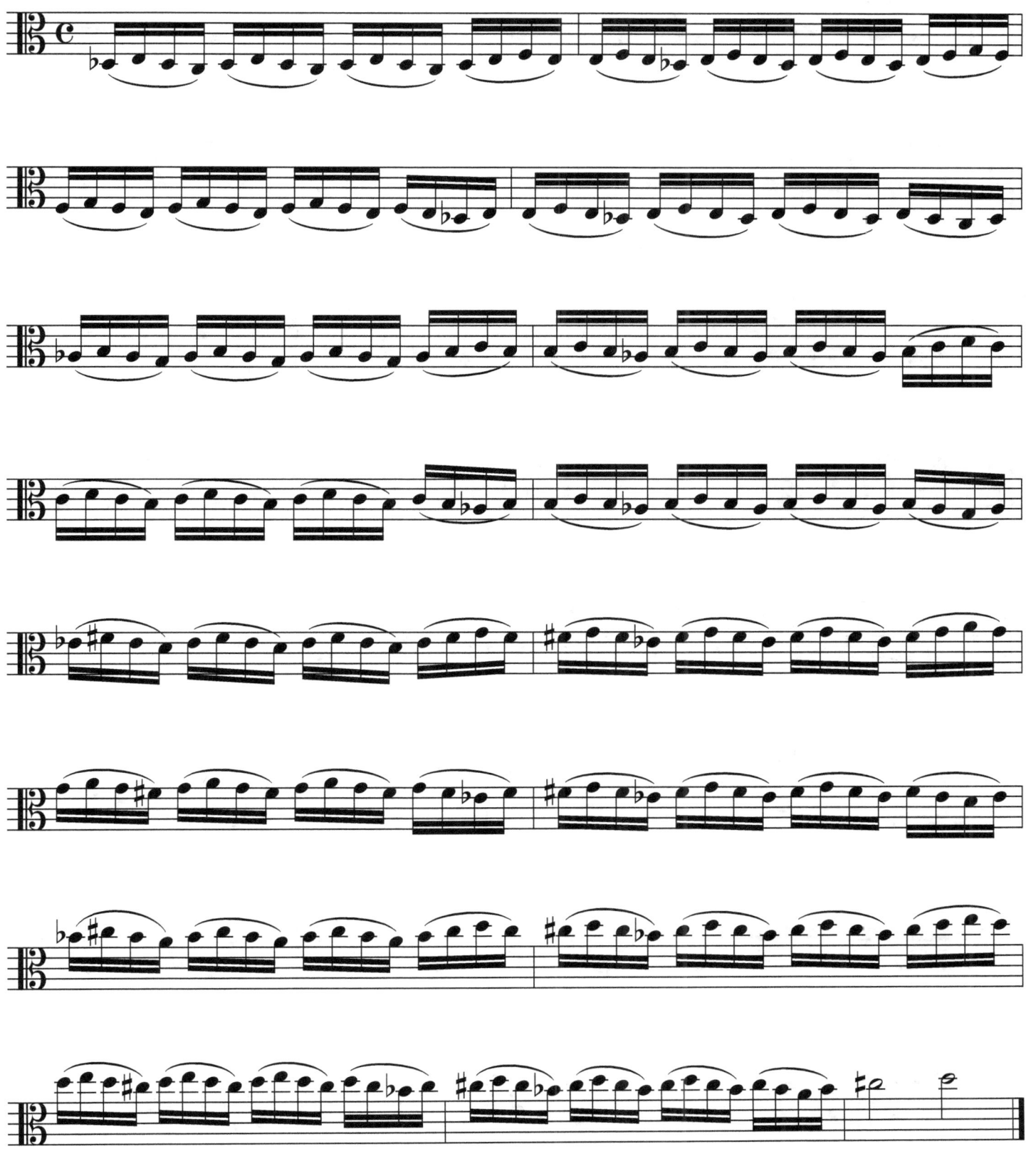

48

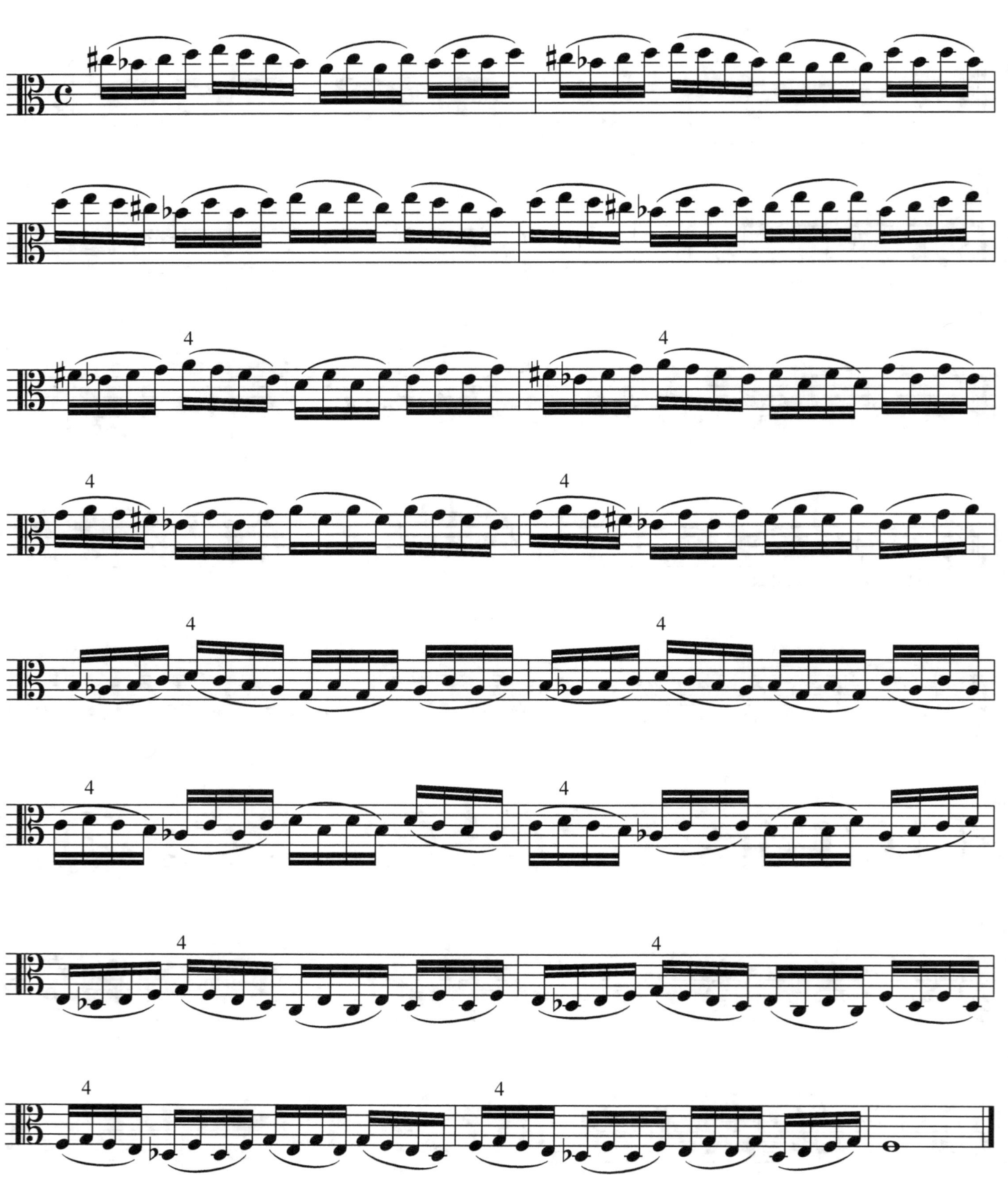

Finger Exercises for the Viola, Book Two

49

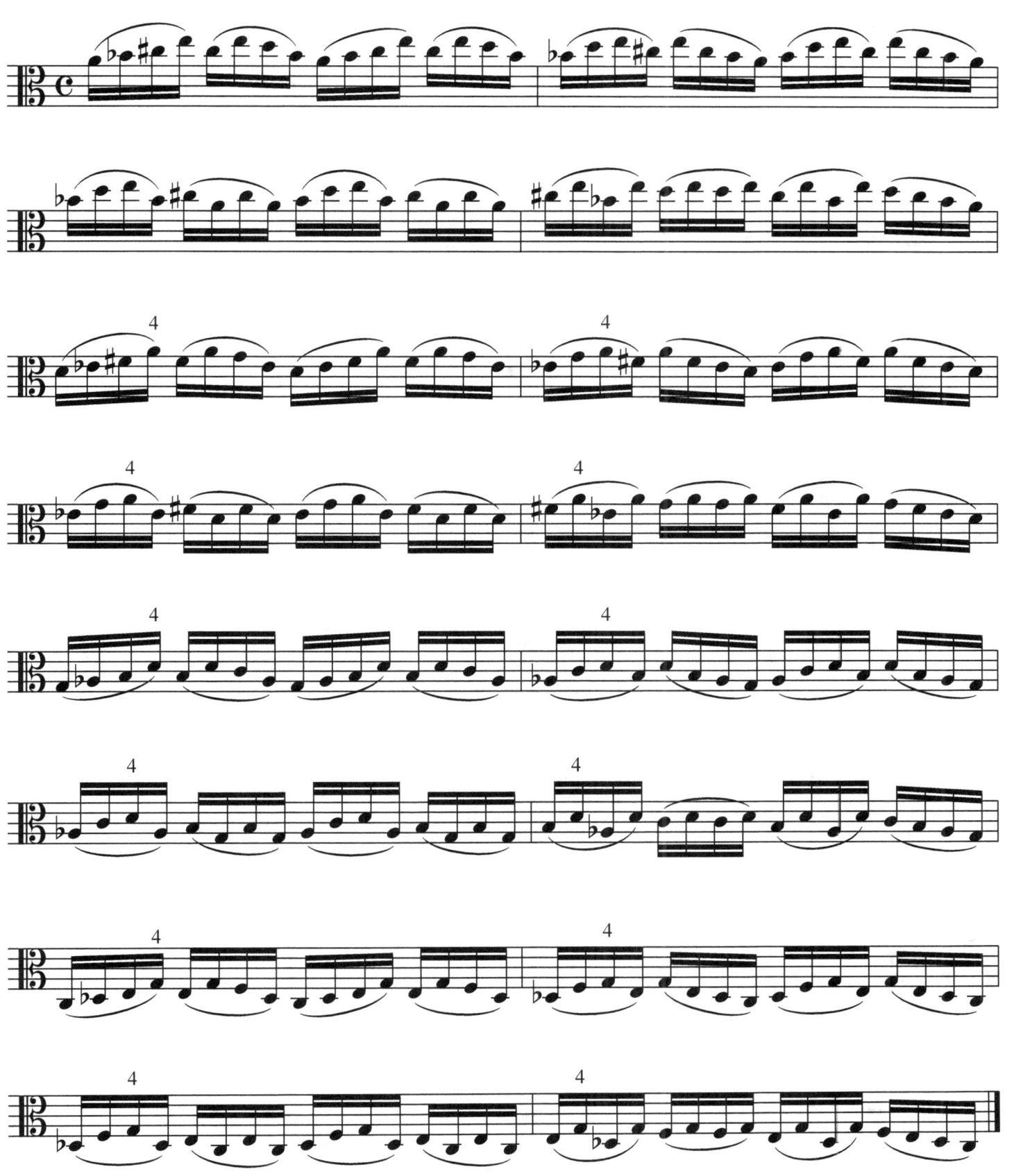

©2018 C. Harvey Publications All Rights Reserved.

50

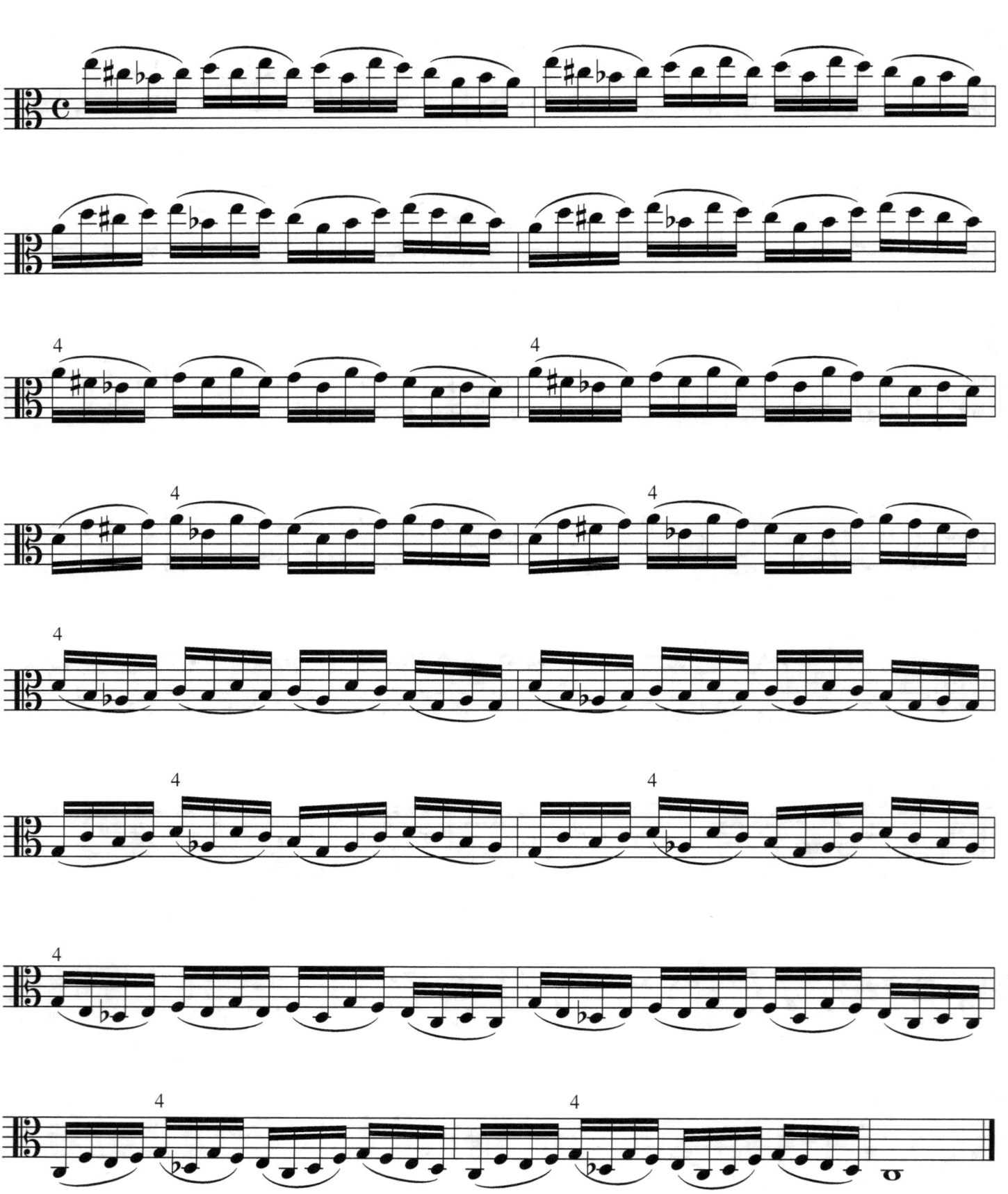

Finger Exercises for the Viola, Book Two

51

Low and High Fourth Finger

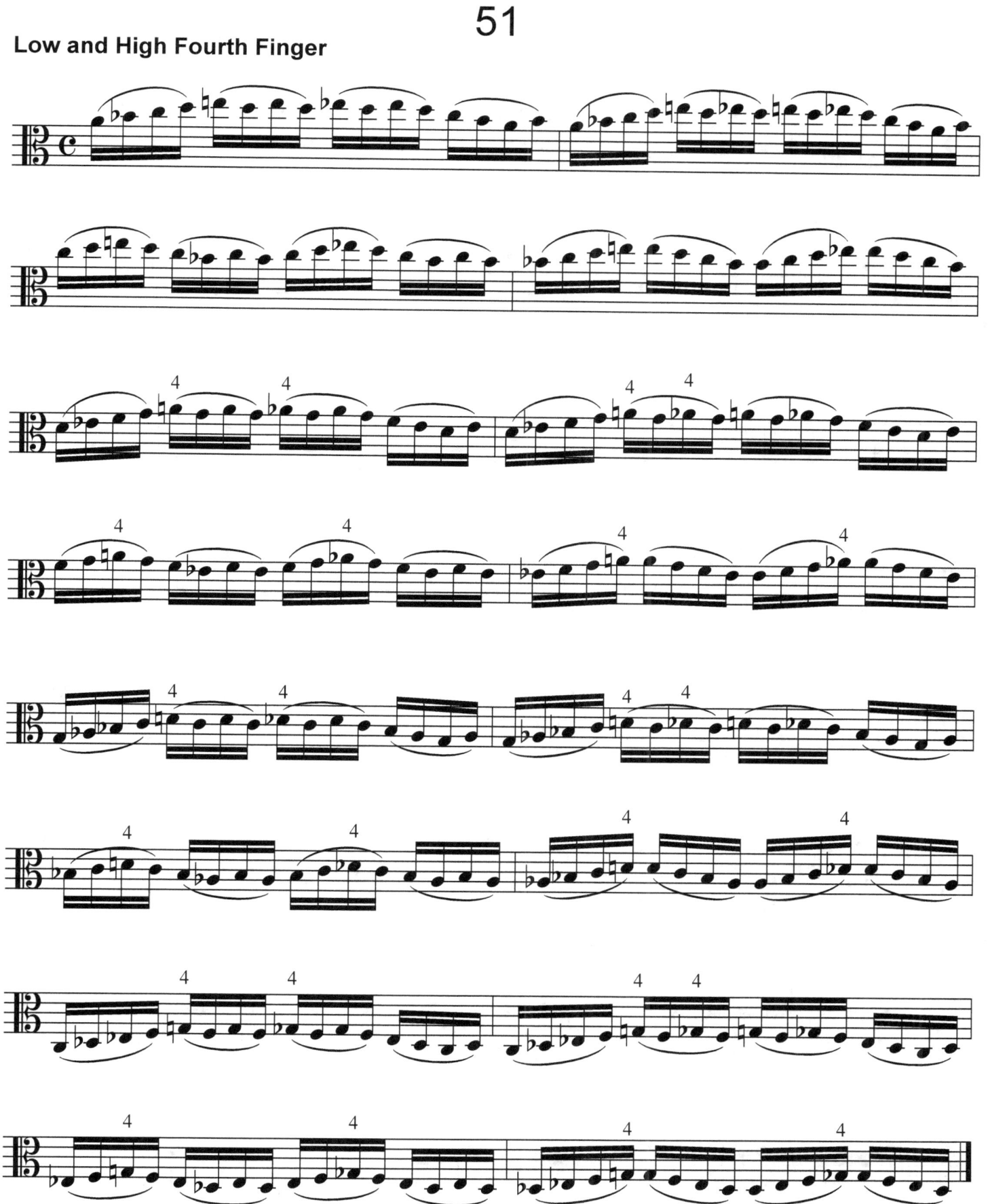

52

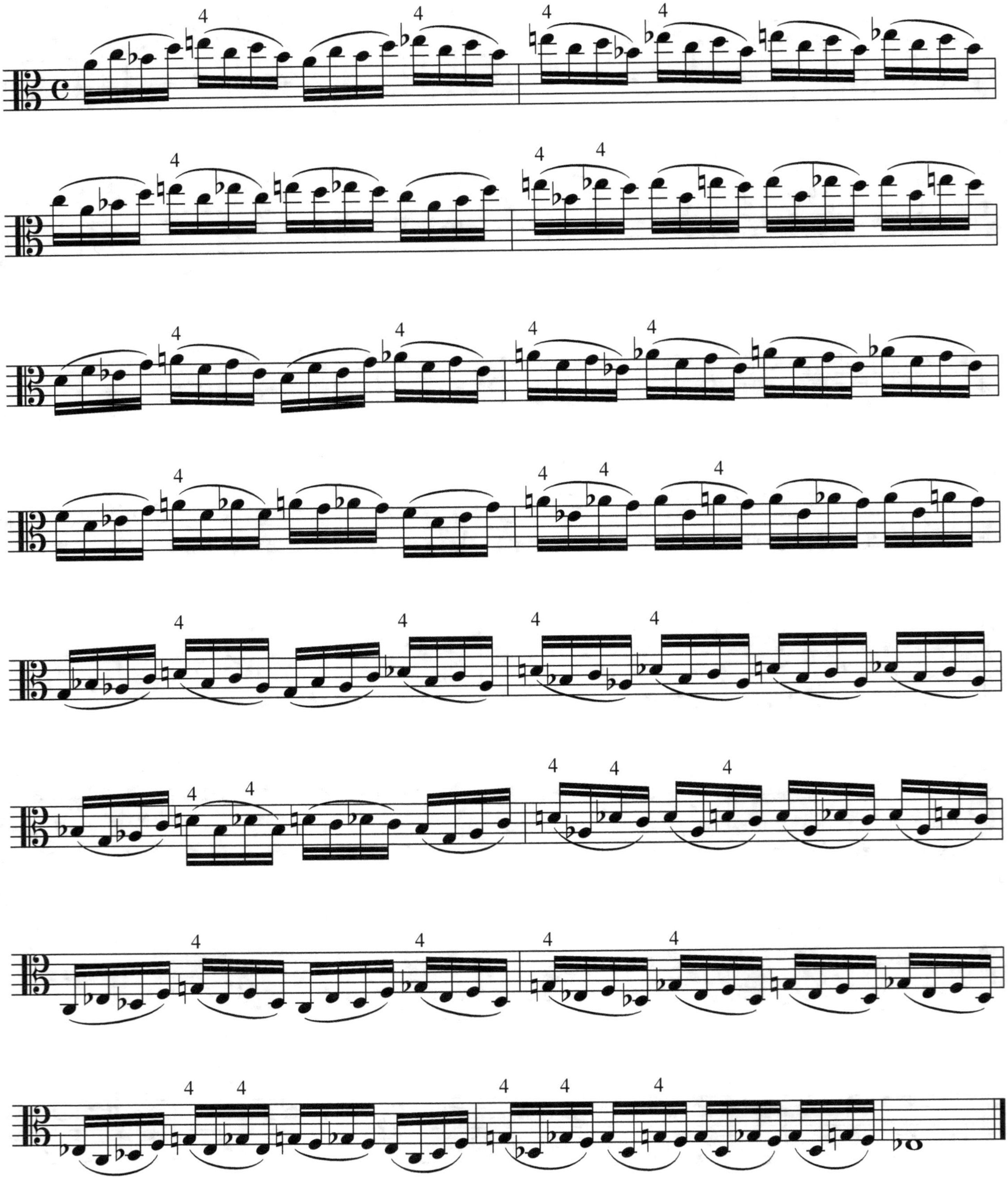

Finger Exercises for the Viola, Book Two

53

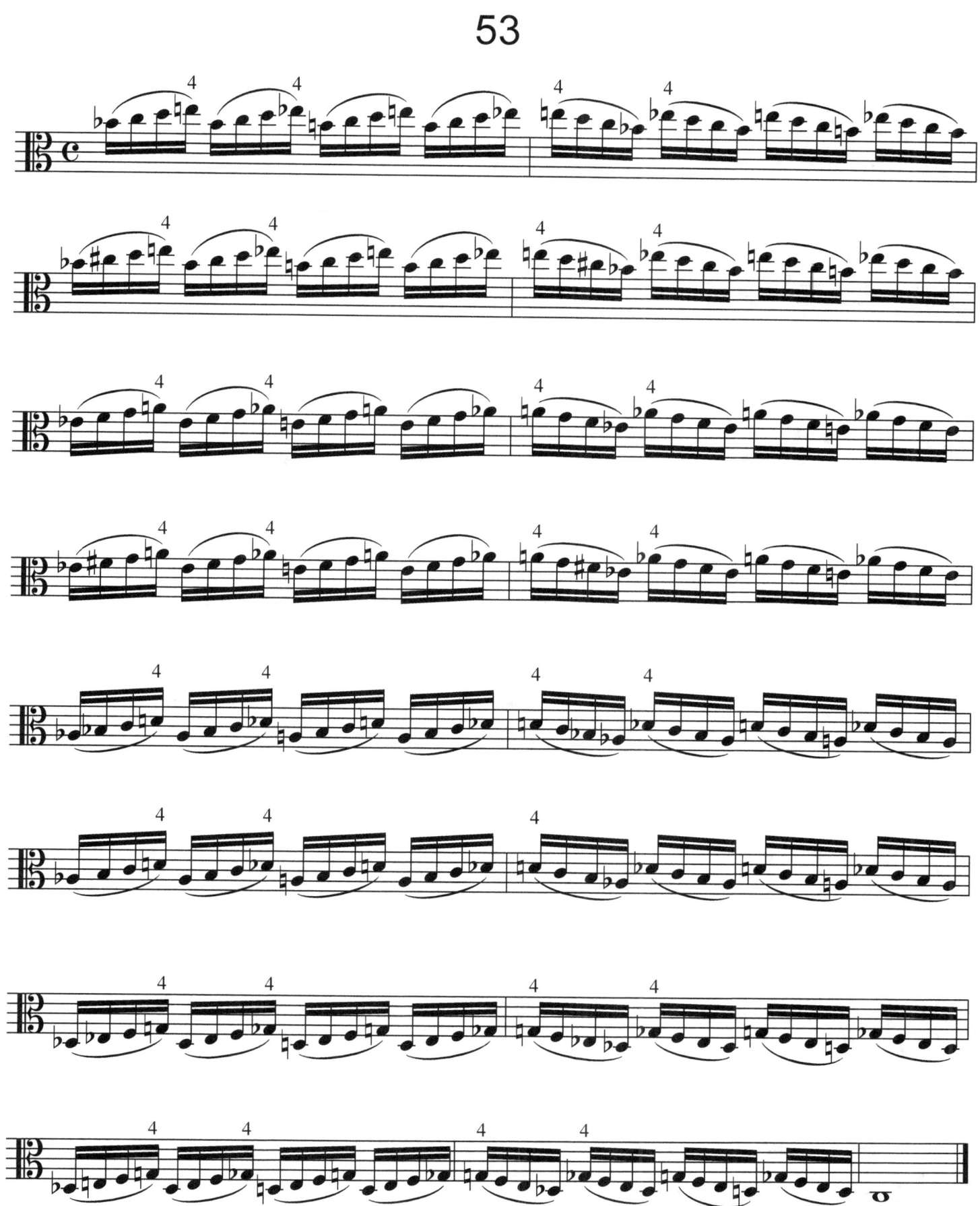

54

Finger Exercises for the Viola, Book Two

55

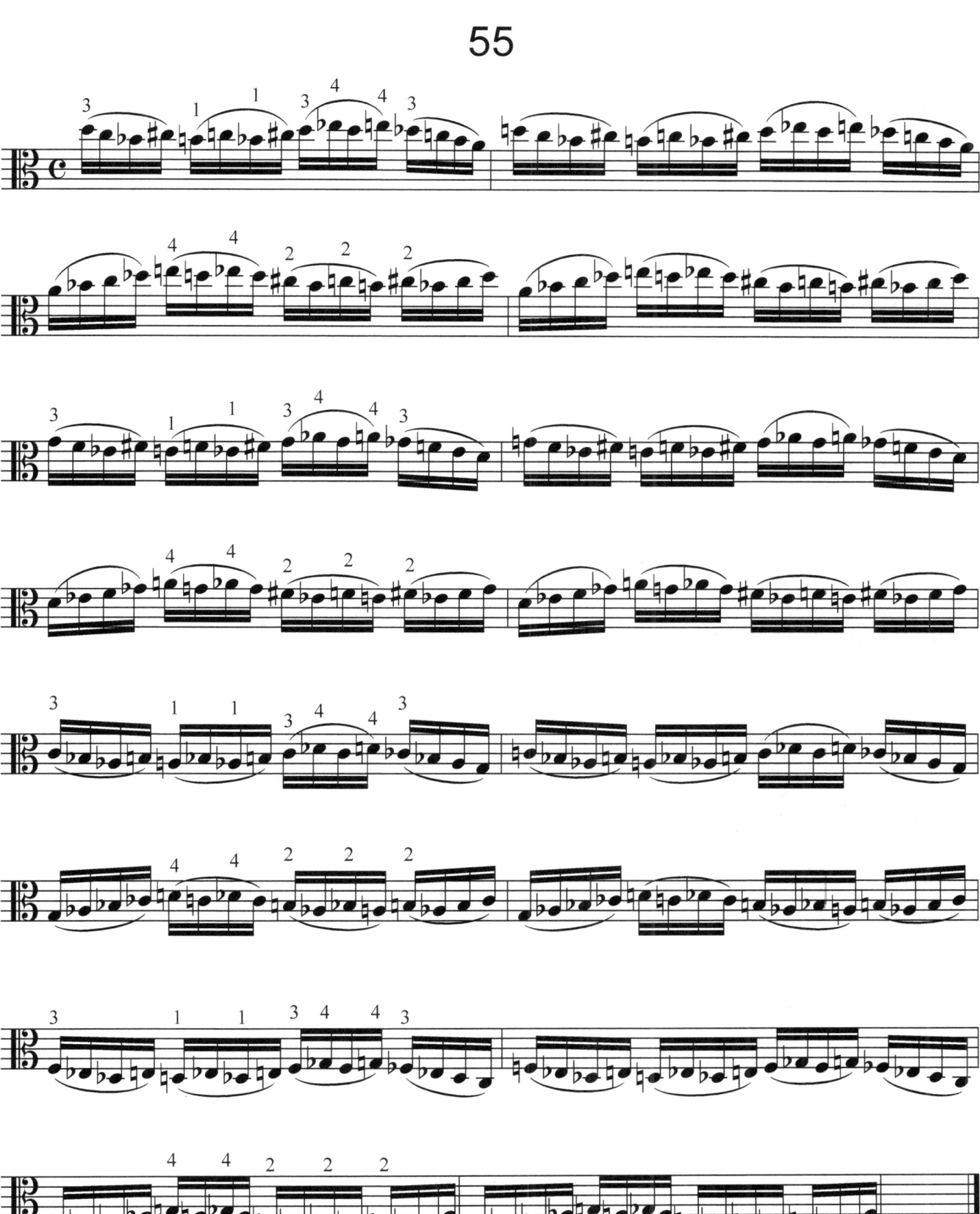

C Major Shifting for the Viola
1
Cassia Harvey

©2014 C. Harvey Publications All Rights Reserved.

www.ingramcontent.com/pod-product-compliance
Lightning Source LLC
Chambersburg PA
CBHW051424070526
44584CB00023B/3564